ARGENTINA
the culture

Greg Nickles

A Bobbie Kalman Book

The Lands, Peoples, and Cultures Series

Crabtree Publishing Company

www.crabtreebooks.com

The Lands, Peoples, and Cultures Series

Created by Bobbie Kalman

Coordinating editor
Ellen Rodger

Project development, photo research, and design
First Folio Resource Group, Inc.
Erinn Banting
Pauline Beggs
Tom Dart
Kathryn Lane
Alana Perez
Debbie Smith

Editing
Jessica Rudolph

Separations and film
Embassy Graphics

Printer
Worzalla Publishing

Consultants
Pampa Risso Patrón, Pan American Cultural Exchange, Houston, Texas; Roberto Risso Patrón; Diana Pelenur, Consulate General of the Republic of Argentina in Montreal

Photographs
Archive Photos: p. 29 (top); Christophe Bluntzer/Impact: p. 23 (top); Corbis/AFP: p. 11 (right); Corbis/Archivo Iconografico S.A.: p. 24 (top); Corbis/Jonathan Blair: p. 29 (bottom); Corbis/Pablo Corral V: p. 9 (bottom), p. 21 (top); Corbis/Abbie Enock,
Travel Ink: p. 24 (bottom); Corbis/Miki Kratsman: p. 13 (right); Corbis/Enzo & Paolo Ragazzini: p. 7 (bottom); Corbis/Reuters Newmedia Inc.: p. 10 (left); Corbis/Hubert Stadler: p. 5 (bottom), p. 9 (top), p. 10 (right), p. 14, p. 16, p. 28; Corbis/Robert van der Hilst: p. 3; Walter Echazú/Infoto: p. 12 (right); Robert Frerck/Odyssey Productions: p. 17 (top); Robert Fried/DDB Stock Photo: p. 6 (left); Pablo Garber: p. 15 (left); Beryl Goldberg: p. 27 (top); Carlos Goldin/DDB Stock Photo: cover, p. 22; Hugo Lazaridis/ LZ Producciones: p. 21 (bottom); Carolina Lescano/Infoto: p. 18 (right); Michael Moody/DDB Stock Photo: p. 5 (top); Graciela Pace/LZ Producciones: p. 12 (left); Julio Pantoja/Infoto: title page, p. 4 (bottom), p. 19 (both), p. 20 (bottom); Daniel Rivademar/ Odyssey Productions: p. 17 (bottom); Nestor Troncoso/LZ Producciones: p. 8, p. 25 (both); Leonardo Zavattaro/LZ Producciones: p. 4 (top), p. 6 (right), p. 7 (top), p. 11 (left), p. 13 (left), p. 15 (right), p. 18 (left), p. 20 (top), p. 23 (bottom), p. 26 , p. 27 (bottom)

Illustrations
Dianne Eastman: icon
Marie Lafrance: pp. 30-31
David Wysotski, Allure Illustrations: back cover

Cover: Two tango dancers perform outside a colorful building in La Boca, in Buenos Aires.

Title page: A musician plays a *quena*, or flute, in Tucumán, in northern Argentina.

Icon: A *bandoneón*, a popular instrument in Argentina, appears at the head of each section.

Back cover: The nine-banded armadillo is protected by armor made up of nine individual plates, or sections.

Published by
Crabtree Publishing Company

PMB 16A
350 Fifth Avenue
Suite 3308
New York
N.Y. 10118

612 Welland Avenue
St. Catharines
Ontario, Canada
L2M 5V6

73 Lime Walk
Headington
Oxford OX3 7AD
United Kingdom

Cataloging in Publication Data
Nickles, Greg, 1969-
    Argentina: the culture/Greg Nickles.
    p.cm. -- (The Lands, peoples, and cultures series)
Includes index.
    ISBN 0-86505-246-8 (RLB) -- ISBN 0-86505-326-X (pbk.)
    1. Argentina--Civilization--Juvenile literature.   [1.
Argentina--Social life and customs.]   I. Title. II. Series.
F2810 .N53 2000
982--dc21

00-043223
LC

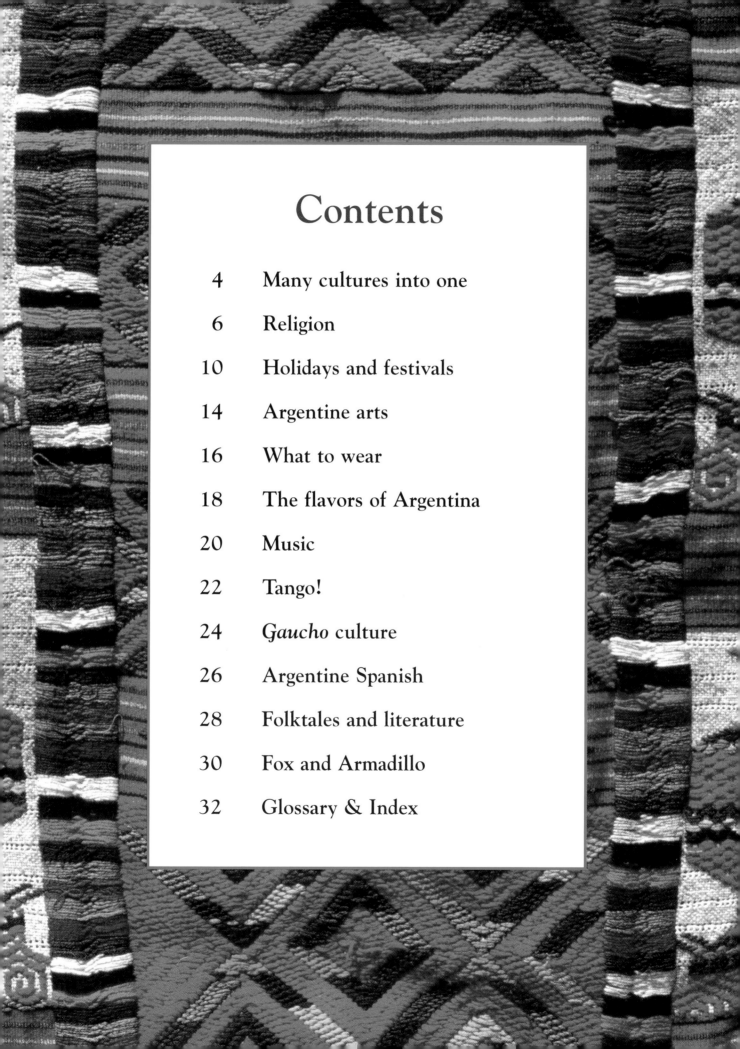

Contents

Many cultures into one

Argentina's culture is a rich mix of many traditions. The country's arts, festivals, food, language, and clothing reflect the different peoples who settled there over time. These include the Native Argentines, who have lived on the land for thousands of years, as well as people who **immigrated** from Europe, the Middle East, Asia, and other parts of South America in the last 500 years.

A man reads the newspaper and enjoys a cup of coffee on his lunch break.

From Europe to South America

Of all the Spanish-speaking nations in **Latin America,** Argentina has some of the strongest ties to Europe. Spain, which ruled the land from the 1500s to the 1800s, introduced its culture to the area. More recent immigrants from Italy, Britain, France, and Germany have also passed along their traditions. Their European styles have influenced Argentina's arts and festivals. Even the streets of the **capital,** Buenos Aires, look and feel like those of a city in Europe.

Native–Argentine influences

Native Argentines once lived throughout the land, but by the 1900s, most of them had been killed by soldiers, European settlers, and disease. Those Native peoples who survive in the isolated parts of the country still celebrate their traditional cultures today. Some Native customs have become part of the Argentine way of life.

*Children, covered in **nieve loca,** or "crazy snow," participate in a parade during the Festival de Pachamama, or Festival of Mother Earth.*

(above) Folk dancers in traditional costume perform one of Argentina's national dances, **El Pericon,** *at a rodeo in the Pampas.*

(below) Musicians play typical South American instruments at a festival in northwest Argentina.

About 90 percent of Argentines are Roman Catholics. Roman Catholicism is a **denomination** of Christianity, the religion based on the teachings of Jesus Christ. Christians believe that Jesus was the son of God sent to earth. They also believe that he was able to perform miracles, such as healing illnesses and returning to life after he was crucified, or put to death on a cross. Jesus' teachings are written in the New Testament, a Christian holy book.

In Argentina today, about a million people are Protestants. Protestantism is another denomination of Christianity. About 500,000 people are Jews. They live by the teachings of their holy book, called the Torah. A few hundred thousand people follow Islam, a religion based on the teachings of the **prophet** Muhammad. Several thousand Native Argentines observe their own traditional beliefs.

Practicing their faith

Explorers from Spain first introduced Christianity to the area in the 1500s. In the following centuries, millions of Roman Catholic settlers from Spain and Italy made the church even stronger in Argentina. Today, 50 percent of Roman Catholics in Argentina go to church on a regular basis, while the rest only attend for major religious holidays or special occasions such as marriages, baptisms, and first communions.

During a baptism, the **priest** gently pours holy water over a baby's head, welcoming him or her into the Church. At the age of ten or eleven, children take part in their first communion, a major Roman Catholic ceremony. During communion, they share holy bread, called the host, that is blessed by the priest. Older children renew their commitment to their faith in a confirmation ceremony.

(left) *This synagogue, or place of Jewish worship and study, is in Buenos Aires. Argentina is home to a small Jewish community.*

(below) *A Roman Catholic priest performs a baptism.*

A statue of the Virgin Mary is brought by cart to the main square of Luján for a procession that marks the end of the yearly pilgrimage.

On a pilgrimage

A pilgrimage is an important journey to a holy site. Each year, thousands of Roman Catholics journey by foot to the Argentine town of Luján. There, they worship in the **basilica** that houses a special statue of the Virgin Mary, the mother of Jesus Christ. According to legend, the statue was being carried by ox cart past its current location one day in 1630. The ox cart got stuck in mud. No one could get it rolling again until the statue was removed. People interpreted this as a sign from the Virgin Mary that her statue should stay where it was. The entire town of Luján and its grand basilica were built around this spot.

Paying respect

Roman Catholics throughout Argentina pay respect to religious figures in return for protection or good fortune. They pray and leave **offerings** for **saints** and heroes at **shrines**. Many shrines in Argentina are built for La Difunta Correa, a woman who is said to have died of thirst in the desert but whose nursing baby miraculously survived.

A shop owner has set up an area in his store where customers can leave gifts of fruits and vegetables for La Difunta Correa.

Native Argentine religions

Some Native Argentines follow the traditional religions of their ancestors. They often mix these beliefs with Roman Catholicism. For example, the Diaguita people of northwest Argentina have festivals for their traditional gods, who include *Inti*, the Sun, *Mama Hilla*, the Moon, and *Pachamama,* the Earth goddess. The Mapuche people of western Argentina believe that the world is balanced between forces of *Ngenechen*, or creation, and *Wakufu*, or destruction. Both the Diaguita and Mapuche also worship the Christian God.

Pachamama is an important goddess for several Native peoples in the Andes mountains. Many stories tell of her power to bring good crops and protect travelers. In return for *Pachamama's* help, worshipers bury **coca** leaves and other offerings for her, and honor her with special festivals. The Mapuche honor their gods during their annual Nquillatún festival. The purpose of this three-day celebration is to show their gratitude for good lands and harvests.

Jesuit missionaries

In the early 1600s, Jesuit missionaries came to live among the northern Native peoples. They believed it was their duty to travel the world and teach people about Christianity. Some local peoples did not welcome them, but others became converts, new followers of the religion. With these converts, the Jesuits built communities called missions where both priests and converts lived.

The missions thrived until 1767, when the kings of Spain and Portugal forced the Jesuits to abandon them. Today, people have mixed opinions of the missionaries. Some think that they helped Native peoples by teaching them how to work the fields, but others feel that the missionaries forced people to work for them and to change their religion.

A woman rests outside a local church in Iruya, in northern Argentina.

(above) The most famous Jesuit ruins are in San Ignacio Miní, in northeast Argentina. There, archways, sculptures, and artwork from the former Jesuit settlement still stand.

(left) The Cathedral of Buenos Aires, one of the largest Roman Catholic churches in Argentina, is located in the center of Buenos Aires.

Holidays and festivals

Argentines have many different holidays and festivals throughout the year. They range from solemn religious events to huge street parties that celebrate national heroes, important historic dates, the harvest, and the arts. The largest holidays are observed across the country, but many smaller holidays are celebrated only in certain towns or regions.

Carnival

In Argentina, as in many other places where Roman Catholicism is a major religion, Carnival is a large festival. It is the celebration, in February or March, that leads up to Lent, a six-week period when Roman Catholics **fast**. Lent prepares them for the Easter holiday, which marks the death of Christ and his return to life.

Carnival is famous for its rich foods, music-filled parades, and brightly colored costumes. Both children and adults dress up as animals, clowns, or cartoon characters. A more modern Carnival tradition that children love is to lie in wait with water balloons, which they throw at passers-by. Fortunately, most victims just laugh after they recover from the surprise of being drenched!

(above) A woman dressed in a colorful costume is one of the thousands of dancers and performers who participate in Carnival festivals across Argentina each year.

(right) Christmas decorations line the Galería Pacífico shopping mall in Buenos Aires, on a sunny December day.

Christmas

On December 25, Christians celebrate Christmas to mark the birth of Jesus Christ. Families put up a Christmas tree, send greeting cards, and wait for Papá Noel, the Argentine Santa Claus, to come with presents. Argentina lies in the southern half of the world, where the seasons are the reverse of those in the north, so December 25 falls in the middle of the summer — when there is never any snow!

Argentina's Christmas season lasts for two weeks. The celebrations begin on Christmas Eve. In the late evening, families go to church for Midnight **Mass**. Afterwards, people enjoy a late supper and special treats such as candied almonds, apple cider, and *pan dulce*, a sweet bread made with nuts. Papá Noel visits while the family is having supper, but the children must wait until midnight to open their gifts.

(below) Children in Salta eagerly await their gifts at a Day of Kings celebration.

(above) A favorite celebration in Buenos Aires happens on the last work day of the year. People throw old papers out of their office windows in preparation for the new year.

The Day of Kings

The Day of Kings, on January 6, is one of the last celebrations of the Christmas season. It honors the New Testament story about three kings who visited the infant Jesus. Before children go to bed on January 5, they leave their best shoes on their windowsills or outside the front door, along with cookies for the kings and water for their camels. They hope that the kings will visit in the night, accept the treats, and leave small gifts in the shoes.

Celebrating the Miracle of Salta

During September, people in and around the northern city of Salta hold the Fiesta del Milagro. This festival celebrates an important statue of Christ that stands in the local cathedral. It is said that in 1592, after the ship carrying it sank, the statue miraculously floated to the shore, where it was found and taken to Salta. Somehow, people forgot about the statue until, a century later, a priest dreamed of it during a series of earthquakes. Believing his dream was a message from God, the priest asked people to find the statue and parade it through the streets. Soon, the earthquakes stopped. To honor this miracle, residents of Salta have paraded the statue through the streets once a year ever since.

Patriotic holidays

Many historic events are honored in Argentina. Two main holidays mark the country's independence. On May 25, people celebrate the Anniversary of the Revolution, the day in 1810 when Argentines began their battle for freedom from Spanish rule. Independence Day, on July 9, is the anniversary of the country's full independence in 1816. Both days are national holidays, celebrated with parades, political speeches, and a day off work.

(above) Thousands of people crowd the main square of Salta. They are about to parade down the streets with the statue of Christ at the Fiesta del Milagro.

(left) Soldiers from the cavalry march through Plaza de Mayo, in Buenos Aires, in honor of Argentina's Independence Day.

A confectioner, or someone who makes candy, pours chocolate into molds to prepare for the Snow Festival in Bariloche.

People leave flowers at the gravesite of Carlos Gardel, a famous tango singer, in Chacarita Cemetery in Buenos Aires.

Snow and chocolate

Bariloche is a southern town that sits high in the Andes mountains. Known for its chocolate and Swiss-style buildings, Bariloche holds a Snow Festival each August. During the festival, there are concerts and a snowman-building competition, as well as a pageant to crown a Queen of Snow and Queen of Chocolate.

From Wales to Argentina

About a century ago, settlers moved from Wales, in Britain, to southern Argentina. Today, their **descendants** keep alive their **heritage** by holding festivals called *eisteddfodds*. The entire community turns out for an *eisteddfodd* to enjoy traditional Welsh music, dancing, singing, poetry, and storytelling. Between performances, people drink Welsh tea and browse through the arts and crafts of local **artisans**.

Celebrating past heroes

Some of Argentina's most beloved heroes, artists, and leaders are celebrated with special holidays each year on the anniversaries of their deaths. Visitors flock to the cemeteries where their heroes are buried to lay flowers at their gravesites.

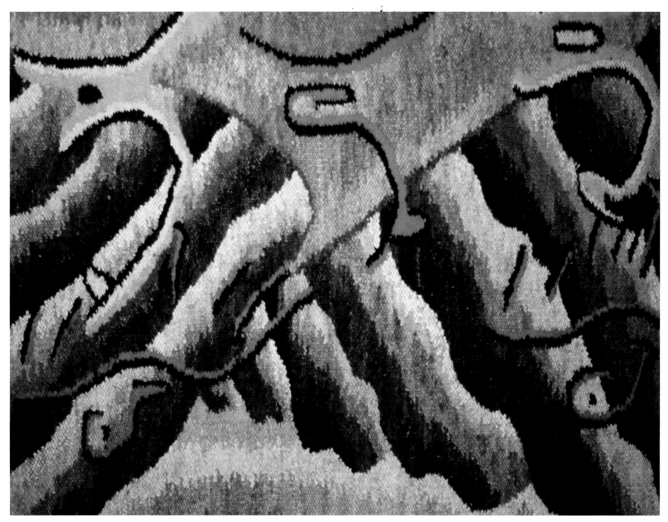

 # Argentine arts

Argentina's first artists were Native peoples who made ceramics, woodcarvings, metalwork, and other crafts. They created everyday objects, as well as items for special occasions. Their decorations were based on their religions and on stories passed down from generation to generation. Beginning in the 1500s, Roman Catholic religious subjects, such as scenes from the New Testament, became common in Argentine artwork. By the 1800s, artists in Argentina began to express their own identity and to show their country in their work.

(top) Weaving brightly colored tapestries with intricate designs is a traditional Argentine art form.

Native arts

Native artisans in northern Argentina often use the same art forms that their ancestors did. For example, the artisans of the Mataco people are known for their fine carvings of birds and animals. They use woods that are naturally green, red, brown, black, or yellow and decorate them with small pieces of bone.

Other popular items that Native artisans make include the special cup and straw used to drink *mate,* a favorite Argentine drink. The traditional cup is made from a **gourd** that is decorated with gold or silver, though some are made entirely of precious metals. Straws called *bombillas* are often made of gold or silver, too, and are finely decorated.

Painting and more

Some of the earliest paintings of Argentine subjects were scenes of the local cowboys, called *gauchos*, who rode the plains. Such paintings were created by Prilidiano Pueyrredón (1823-70), who many consider to be the country's first major painter. Other artists followed with realistic-looking scenes of Argentine life.

Since the late nineteenth century, Argentine artists have explored all sorts of styles. Many traveled to Europe and returned to Argentina with new experiences and ideas. Cándido López (1840-1902) painted large, detailed pictures of war. Antonio Berni (1905-81) created murals and other paintings that portrayed a life of poverty. Today's established artists include Luis Benedit, Guillermo Kuitca, and Alfredo Prior. They are known for painting unusual, distorted pictures of everyday objects.

Art in La Boca

La Boca, in Buenos Aires, is one of the most famous neighborhoods in all of Argentina. Originally the home of many Italian immigrants and their families, La Boca was where Argentine painter Quinquela Martín grew up in the 1900s. His famous colorful paintings of the port and its workers encouraged people in the neighborhood to paint their houses as they appeared in his paintings, in brilliant greens, blues, yellows, and reds.

Today, La Boca is home to many artists, including dancers, musicians, painters, sculptors, and photographers. The neighborhood also has an outdoor artists' market.

From fear to celebration

In 1976, Argentina's military took control of the government. In the years following, it would not allow people to express their opinions. It imprisoned and even murdered thousands of Argentines. Many people, including many important artists, fled the country for fear of their lives.

Freedom of speech was restored in 1983, when the military government gave up power and elections were held. As a result, thousands of people, including artists, returned from abroad, bringing their fresh, exciting ideas back to Argentina's arts scene.

(above) Students in Buenos Aires paint a mural on one of their school's walls.

(left) A metalworker carefully carves decorations onto a silver cup for mate.

15

Most of the time, Argentines wear clothes like those worn in North America or Europe. Pants, shirts, sweaters, blouses, jackets, dresses, and skirts are all common. Traditional costumes are worn on special occasions, though some groups in the remote parts of the countryside wear them more often.

Ponchos

A poncho is one of the most common types of traditional clothing in Argentina. It is a very simple, large rectangular cloth with a slit in the middle for the head. A very good poncho may be woven by hand from the wool of a *vicuña*, an animal related to a camel. Many colors are used to create beautiful patterns. The colors and design can identify the region where the person wearing the poncho lives.

Once worn by legendary heroes, ponchos today are mostly worn by people in the countryside. Ponchos are also worn as part of traditional costumes at celebrations. There is even a poncho festival in the northern town of Catamarca, where many are made.

Make a poncho

Ask an adult to help you make a poncho. You will need:

- an old blanket that you are allowed to cut up
- a tape measure
- masking tape or Scotch tape
- scissors
- colored yarn and a large needle
- fabric paint (optional)

A vendor at an outdoor market in Tucumán, in northwest Argentina, sells ponchos, hats, and leather belts.

Instructions:
1. Fold the blanket in half lengthwise.

2. Measure along the folded side to find the center. Mark it with a small piece of tape.

3. Measure along the fold 6 inches (15 cm) on each side of the center, and mark with tape. Remove the tape in the center.

4. Carefully make a hole for your head by cutting along the fold from one piece of tape to the other.

5. Remove the tape and put the poncho over your head. If the poncho is too wide or too long, trim it.

6. To keep the blanket from fraying around the hole, thread the needle with yarn and stitch around the cut edge. If you like, you can stitch all the way around the poncho's outer edge, too.

7. Decorate your new poncho with different colors of yarn or fabric paint.

Native Argentine style

For centuries, Argentina's Native peoples have woven fine, warm fabrics from the soft wool of sheep and other local animals, such as vicuñas and alpacas. They dye the fabrics in natural dyes and use them to make ponchos as well as other clothing, blankets, and wall hangings.

Second skins

For hundreds of years, leather, one of Argentina's major products, has been used to make clothing. Today, skilled leatherworkers make beautiful shoes, boots, coats, and purses. Not all leatherworkers have always been this skilled. The *gauchos* used to make leather boots from the hides of a young horse's legs simply by slipping the skins over their own feet and wearing them until they dried!

(right) Two children dress in pants, a T-shirt, and a sweater on a fall day in Buenos Aires.

(below) A woman works at a loom, weaving bright fabrics out of wool.

The flavors of Argentina

Argentina's food is strongly influenced by European cooking. Each group of immigrants brought their favorite foods and recipes to their new country. Today, the foods of all these nationalities are eaten throughout Argentina. Italian foods, such as ravioli, lasagna, spaghetti, and pizza, are especially popular.

Meat and more meat

Argentines eat a lot of meat, especially beef. It is not unusual for people to dine on beef twice a day. The *gauchos* are said to eat nothing but beef for weeks on end while they are out on the range, tending their herds. Favorite beef dishes include *carbonada criolla,* which is made with minced beef, and *bife a caballo,* or "beef on horseback," which is a steak topped with a fried egg. *Pucheros,* or stews usually made with chicken and vegetables, and *locros*, or stews of Native origin made with corn, sausage, and vegetables are also popular.

A chef bakes empanadas *in a clay oven. These turnovers, stuffed with ground meat, eggs, vegetables, or fish, are a favorite Argentine dish.*

Roasting over the fire

Family and community gatherings in Argentina are marked with a special barbecue called an *asado.* Argentina's president even holds *asados* for foreign leaders. An *asado* is much larger than the average barbecue in North America. It requires an open-air roasting pit, a large fire with hot coals, and huge cuts of meat that are roasted whole on a spit. Guests talk, drink, play games and music, and dance as they wait for their meal to cook. Then, the roasted meat is served by slicing it right off the skewer.

Wine

Argentines are wine lovers, and have built one of the world's largest wine-making industries. Each year, thousands of people from all over the country come to hand-pick the grapes in the **vineyards** of Mendoza, San Juan, Salta, and La Rioja. Once the harvest is over and the juices are squeezed from the grapes to make wine, there are many festivals and parties.

Huge sides of beef are roasted over hot coals at an asado.

Sweet treats

Many Argentines have a sweet tooth. Treats such as *dulce de leche,* a sweet, milky spread that is eaten like jam, and special *alfajores,* or cookies, are very popular.

With an adult, you can make the same sweet "sandwich" cookies that Argentines enjoy. *Alfajores* wafers are traditionally eaten with *dulce de leche* spread between them. If your local store does not have *dulce de leche,* you can use jam.

What you need:
- 2/3 pound (300 grams) butter
- 1 cup (250 milliliters) each of granulated white sugar, unbleached flour, and ground almonds
- 1/2 tsp. (2 milliliters) vanilla extract
- 1/2 tsp. (2 milliliters) almond extract
- 3 eggs
- 1 cup (250 milliliters) jam (or *dulce de leche,* if you can find it)
- a large bowl and large spoon
- a tea towel
- a cookie sheet
- a rolling pin
- a round cookie cutter (a small, clean jar will do)

What to do:

1. Combine the butter, sugar, and vanilla and almond extracts in the bowl. Beat.

2. Add the eggs, flour, and almonds. Mix the dough thoroughly.

3. Cover the bowl with a tea towel and place it in the refrigerator for half an hour.

4. Preheat the oven to 350° Fahrenheit (180° Celsius). Grease and flour the cookie sheet.

5. On a lightly floured surface, roll out the dough to just over 1/4 inch (1/2 centimeter) thick. Cut as many circles as you can with the cookie cutter.

6. Place the circles of dough on the cookie sheet, being careful not to crowd them. Bake for 15-20 minutes or until the edges turn golden.

7. Once the cookies cool, spread jam or *dulce de leche* on half of them. Put a second cookie on top of each to make a "sandwich."

A baker stands near a basket of bread in her pastry shop in Bariloche, southern Argentina.

Music

In Argentina, music floats in the streets and in homes, as family members play guitar or sing. Musical performances are part of every holiday and festival, and people who live in the city regularly flock to concerts.

There are many styles of music throughout Argentina. Folk music blends Native Argentine and Spanish music with music from other Latin American countries and Africa. Classical music from Europe and Argentine rock music are also very popular.

Folk music

In Argentina, folk singers have entertained people in the cities and countryside for hundreds of years. Their songs tell tales of love and stories from Argentina's history and **folklore**. Accompanying these singers are musicians who play European instruments, such as guitars, flutes, and violins, and traditional Argentine instruments, including the *quena,* or flute, the *charango,* a stringed instrument made from the shell of an armadillo, the *siku,* or pan flute, and *bombos,* or drums.

(above) A guitar player entertains passengers on a bus during a long bus trip.

(below) Mercedes Sosa, a popular Argentine folk singer, performs at a concert in Tucumán, in northwest Argentina.

(above) Performers rehearse the Opera Fidello at the Teatro Colón in Buenos Aires. One of the world's best-known opera houses, it covers an entire city block and has seven stories of balconies.

(right) Antonio Tarrago Ros, a popular tango singer and **bandoneón** player, sings "Verdulera," a favorite song in Argentina.

The bandoneón

One instrument — the *bandoneón* — is more popular than any other instrument in Argentine music. A *bandoneón* is like a small accordion, except that instead of long keys, it has buttons on both sides that are pressed to play notes. Its sound comes from air that is sucked in or squeezed out of **bellows**. A *bandoneón*'s bellows are very large, and can be stretched to surprising lengths before they must be squeezed together again.

Tango!

Of all Argentina's art forms, none is more famous or popular than tango. Tango is both a dramatic dance and a style of music with lively but sad melodies. Its popularity has led some people to say that *My Beloved Buenos Aires*, a well-known tango song, is Argentina's unofficial national anthem.

Argentine audiences and performers take tango very seriously. People regularly spend hours watching tango singers and dancers perform at cafés, restaurants, or in special tango bars. Many ordinary Argentines also tango.

The history of tango

Tango music and dance were invented in La Boca about a hundred years ago. People who worked on the docks played, sang, and danced to it. The words in tango music often described the everyday hardships these people faced.

At first, Argentines outside Buenos Aires did not accept the tango because it did not show their feelings and experiences. Also, many people considered the tango too rough and passionate. By the 1920s, however, the tango spread to the rest of Argentina and Europe and became a huge success. Now, tango musicians and dancers perform around the world, and in Buenos Aires the dance is as popular as ever.

Two tango dancers perform on the streets of La Boca.

22

It takes three to tango

A tango performance is sometimes compared to a short, dramatic play between two dancers and a singer. Spectators sit at small tables around the dance floor waiting for the performers to enter. The show starts with a tango singer, wearing an elegant dress or suit, accompanied by his or her *bandoneón* player. The *bandoneón* is the main instrument for tango, but sometimes a piano, violin, guitar, flute, and **double-bass** join in. Soon, two dancers in fancy clothes appear. Holding one another tightly, they cross the stage, making fast, sharp steps, turns, and dips.

Tango legends

The most famous tango singer of all time is Carlos Gardel, who grew up in Buenos Aires. People around the world still buy and listen to his great recordings, some of which are over 80 years old. Another of tango's greatest musicians was Astor Piazolla (1921-92). He combined traditional tango sounds with jazz and other kinds of music to create tango that is especially popular with younger fans.

Fans of the tango can buy figurines at flea markets in Buenos Aires.

More than tango...

Tango is the best-known form of dance in Argentina, but there are other popular styles. Ballet is enjoyed in the cities, and Welsh dancing is popular at *eistedfodds*. There is also a rich tradition of folk dancing throughout the country. The *zamba,* which dancers perform while holding handkerchiefs, is the best-known folk dance. Its many versions include the *zamba de Vargas,* whose music is said to have changed the outcome of the Battle of Vargas in 1867. According to legend, Argentine troops were near defeat when this tune inspired them to fight on and win.

Until the late 1800s, the *gauchos,* Argentina's legendary cowboys and herdsmen, lived throughout the countryside. They had difficult lives, riding the open plains and herding thousands of horses and cattle to places where they would be sold. Working and camping outdoors for months in the heat and cold, a *gaucho* often owned nothing but his horse, saddle, knife, and the clothes on his back.

Gauchos passed their spare moments singing, dancing, and writing poems. These pastimes had a major influence on Argentina's arts. Many folk dances and songs were influenced by *gauchos.* *Gauchos'* lives became the subjects of paintings, folktales, and poems. On modern ranches and at festivals, today's *gauchos* keep many of their traditions alive.

Snappy dressers

Gauchos' costumes can be very flashy. Balloon trousers, called *bombachas,* are tucked into accordion-shaped leather boots and covered with broad, leather *guardamontes.* The *guardamontes* protect *gauchos'* legs from thorns as they ride through brush. Broad-brimmed hats keeps the sun off *gauchos'* heads and ponchos are worn over simple shirts. Brightly colored woolen *faja* sashes are wrapped around the *gauchos'* waists to protect their backs during long rides. These are sometimes worn with special leather belts called *rastras,* which are covered with silver coins. The *rastras* are reminders of the days when there were no banks and *gauchos* wore money-belts to keep their savings from being lost or stolen.

*(top) In this painting by Juan Manuel Blanes, entitled "Dawn," a **gaucho** begins another busy day on the Pampas.*

(right) Gauchos keep their equipment in tackle boxes on the farms where they live.

(above) A young woman, dressed in traditional **gaucho** costume, plays a drum and sings at a festival in Mendoza, in northern Argentina.

(right) **Gauchos** wear traditional ponchos and uniforms, bordered in black, in honor of General Martín Güemes.

Celebrating gauchos

Several Argentine festivals honor the *gauchos*. The town of San Antonio de Areco, for example, holds an annual Festival of Tradition. *Gauchos* come from all over the country with their families to camp out and take part in the weekend-long celebration. Townspeople and cowboys dress in their finest *gaucho* costumes. In addition to a parade and an enormous *asado*, the festival is filled with *gaucho* poetry, dancing, and traditional games.

The game of *sortija*, a competition where *gauchos* show off their horseriding skills, always attracts a crowd. In *sortija*, a ring that is small enough to fit on a finger is hung high between two tall posts. *Gauchos* on horseback, dressed in their traditional clothing, take turns trying to put a short stick through the ring while riding at full speed. Players are disqualified if they fail after two tries, bend their arms while reaching for the ring, or lose their hat while riding.

The gaucho general

Each year in the city of Salta, *gauchos* gather to honor their dead hero, the Argentine general Martín Güemes. Güemes was a *caudillo*, a regional leader who fought for Argentina's independence from Spain. He was killed in battle in 1821 while leading his troops. On June 16, *gauchos* from the countryside light fires by Güemes's monument in Salta, where they stand guard all night. The next day, on the anniversary of the day Güemes died, they join the people of Salta in honoring the general. All *gauchos* wear black scarves to mourn their fallen hero.

Argentine Spanish

Spanish is Argentina's official language. It was brought to the region by the explorers and immigrants who came to the land from Spain in the 1500s. Nearly all Argentines speak Spanish as their first language, although common second languages include Italian, English, French, German, and Native Argentine languages such as Quechua, Guaraní, and Mapuche.

Not quite like Spain

Argentines have their own kind of Spanish that is different than that in Spain. Argentine Spanish sounds somewhat like Italian. This is because the millions of Italian immigrants who came to Argentina added their own words and pronunciations as they learned to speak the language. Another difference between these two types of Spanish is that Argentines have kept an old-fashioned style of grammar that people in Spain stopped using centuries ago. For example, in Spain people say *tú* to mean "you." Argentines usually use *vos*, which is more formal.

Argentines are also known for adding the word *che* (pronounced "chay") to their sentences to grab the attention of someone they know. When an Argentine calls out, "Che," it means something like, "Hey, buddy," in English.

English	Spanish
yes	*sí*
no	*no*
hello	*hola*
goodbye	*adiós or chau*
see you later	*hasta luego*
good morning	*buenos días*
good afternoon	*buenas tardas*
good evening	*buenas noches*
please	*por favor*
thank you	*gracias*
you're welcome	*de nada*
excuse me	*disculpe*
How do you do?	*¿Mucho gusto?*
I don't understand.	*No entiendo.*

(below) These children have lots of picture books to choose from in their neighborhood bookstore.

26

Living with *lunfardo*

Many people in Buenos Aires use *lunfardo* words and expressions in their daily language. *Lunfardo* is a **slang** spoken only in Buenos Aires. A century ago, *lunfardo* was only spoken by criminals who did not want anyone else to understand what they were saying. Over time, it became popular throughout the city. Today, people are becoming interested in *lunfardo* once again. They are hearing it in the words of tango songs, which are becoming more and more popular. There is even a *Lunfardo* Academy of Buenos Aires, which studies the slang.

¿What punctuation is that?

Question marks and exclamation marks are used differently in Spanish than they are in English. Spanish uses two marks for each sentence instead of one. The first mark, which looks upside down to English speakers, appears at the beginning of a sentence. For example, the question "Does Rosa speak Spanish?" in Spanish is written *"¿Rosa habla español?"* The upside-down question mark may also appear in the middle of a sentence, if that is where the question begins, as in *"Rosa habla español, ¿no?"* or "Rosa speaks Spanish, right?"

By looking at the punctuation on this sign can you tell how many questions the leopard is asking?

*A factory worker binds, or puts together, the morning edition of the **Clarin,** a daily newspaper in Argentina.*

CONSEJOS DE MARTÍN FIERRO A SUS HIJOS:

LOS HERMANOS SEAN UNIDOS
PORQUE ESA ES LA LEY PRIMERA
TENGAN UNIÓN VERDADERA,

EN CUALQUIER TIEMPO QUE SEA,
PORQUE SI ENTRE ELLOS PELEAN,
LOS DEVORAN LOS DE "AJUERA".

Folktales and literature

Argentina is a land of folktales, poetry, short stories, novels, and plays. Native-Argentine myths, historical events, *gauchos,* birds, and even imaginary monsters said to live in the far south are all subjects of tales. Many of the country's stories come from the region around Salta, which is sometimes called the Province of Legends.

Tales of the wild frontier

Some of Argentina's favorite folktales and stories are about the *gauchos* and adventurers who lived in the roughest parts of the land before the 1900s. *El Gaucho Martín Fierro,* an **epic** poem studied by every child in school, is the most famous piece of writing about *gaucho* life. Published in two parts by poet José Hernández in 1872 and 1879, it tells of the adventures of a fictional *gaucho* named Martín Fierro.

Just visiting?

Gauchos are not the only cowboys in Argentine stories. Three outlaws called Butch Cassidy, the Sundance Kid, and Etta Place came to Patagonia together in 1901 from the United States, where they were wanted for robbing banks and trains. They continued their criminal careers in Argentina, raiding several banks before leaving in 1905 for neighboring Bolivia. Today, people in Argentina tell stories of the crooks, called them *bandidos Nortamericanos,* or North American bandits. In these tales, the outlaws are not described as criminals, but as heroes who end up on the wrong side of the law.

(top) A tiled mural shows Martín Fierro speaking to a group of gauchos at a ranch in the Pampas.

28

Famous ways with words

Argentina's most famous writer was Jorge Luis Borges, who died in 1986 at the age of 86. Borges was loved around the world for his essays, poems, and short stories, which often told of strange and magical events. His writing vividly described sights that his readers found all the more astounding since Borges had gone blind. Today, his two best-known books are the short-story collections *Fictions* and *El Aleph*.

Manuel Puig and Osvaldo Soriano, both of whom died in the 1990s, are two more of Argentina's internationally known authors. Puig was famous for his novel *Kiss of the Spider Woman*, which told the story of two political prisoners. Because of its **controversial** subject, Puig was forced out of the country in the 1970s by Argentina's military leaders. Soriano, who was popular for his humor, wrote several novels including *Shadows*, an unusual story of an Argentine who is lost in his own country.

Jorge Luis Borge stands outside the **Biblioteca Nacional,** *Argentina's National Library, in Buenos Aires.*

A photograph from the early 1900s shows the Sundance Kid (seated left) and Butch Cassidy (seated right) with their gang, "the wild bunch."

Fox and Armadillo

Argentine folktales began as stories told by Native peoples and by European immigrants. Over the years, these stories have been retold and changed many times. Here is a story about a sly fox and an even smarter armadillo.

The tale of Fox and Armadillo

Fox owned a farm. He never lifted a finger to take care of it, however. Each year, he tricked his neighbors into growing his crops for free. One year, Fox went to visit Armadillo.

Armadillo was sometimes shy — she would roll into a ball when frightened — but she was no fool. She suspected that Fox would try to trick her.

"I will let you grow any crop you like on my land, without rent," Fox offered. "All I ask in return is that you give me half the harvest."

"That seems fair," Armadillo said carefully.

"Do you mind which half you keep?" asked Fox.

"No," Armadillo replied, puzzled.

"Then, I will take the half that grows above the ground," Fox said. His plan was to leave her the worthless roots.

Armadillo saw through Fox's trick and came up with her own plan. She pretended that she had been fooled and agreed to the deal. Sure that he had tricked her, Fox left on vacation to visit his friend Jaguar. When he returned at harvest time expecting to take away Armadillo's crop, he found her storing a great pile of potatoes.

"All that's left in the field are the tops of the potato plants! I can't eat those!" Fox said, surprised. "But you wanted the top half," Armadillo replied. "I'm just following our deal."

Fox was frustrated, but did not suspect that Armadillo knew his trick. "We shall try again next season," he agreed, "but this time I will take the bottom half of the crop, and you will have the top. It is only fair."

That winter was a hungry one for Fox. Next spring, sure that he had fixed his plan, Fox again went on vacation. He returned at harvest time, expecting to feast on Armadillo's potatoes. Instead, he found her storing a crop of wheat.

"What's going on?" he asked. "You didn't say you were planting wheat! I can't eat the stubble and roots that you left!"

"But you wanted the bottom half. I'm just following our deal," Armadillo replied.

Determined to make his trick work, Fox settled on a new idea. "I have been very generous to you, Armadillo, and twice I have not been able to share your crops. Next season I will let you plant again, but you must let me have the top and bottom of the crop. It is only fair."

Armadillo thought a moment, and then asked, "May I have the middle?"

"Of course!" Fox answered, trying not to laugh. "Grow whatever you want, as long as you keep our deal!"

Fox spent another winter hungry and by spring was looking very thin. Again he left for vacation, certain that when he returned, he would feast on Armadillo's harvest. But when he returned, he could not believe his eyes. Armadillo was taking away the last of the cobs of corn.

"What are you doing?" Fox cried.

"Taking my share — the middle," Armadillo replied matter-of-factly.

Fox was enraged. "This is not what I wanted!" he shouted. "I cannot eat cornstalks!"

Armadillo mustered the courage to finally set Fox straight. "Three times you tried to trick me so you could take the food I worked to grow. Three times I gave you the share of the crop you wanted. Believe me, you certainly got what you asked for!"

Fox knew he had been out-tricked, and he was too tired and hungry to argue. The next season he finally did his own planting and never again tried to fool his neighbors into doing his work.

Glossary

artisan A skilled craftsperson

basilica A church given special rights by the pope

bellow A device that produces gusts of air, especially to make the sound of a *bandoneón* or accordion

capital A city where the government of a state or country is located

coca A type of South American shrub. Dried coca leaves are chewed by the Native peoples of Argentina and used to make tea.

controversial Causing a dispute or argument

denomination An organized religious group within a faith

descendant A person who can trace his or her family roots to a certain family or group

double-bass A large, deep-sounding stringed instrument that looks like a violin but is played with one end resting on the floor

epic A long poem or story that tells of heroic deeds

fast To stop eating food or certain kinds of food for religious or health reasons

folklore The traditional beliefs, stories, and customs of a group of people that have been passed down the generations by word of mouth

gourd The hard-shelled fruit of certain vines, which is dried and used to make cups, bowls, and other utensils

heritage Customs, objects, and achievements handed down from earlier generations

immigrate To settle in a different country

Latin America The Spanish-, French-, and Portuguese-speaking countries south of the United States

Mass The main ceremony of the Roman Catholic Church

offering A gift presented to a god as a sign of worship

priest A religious leader

prophet A person who is believed to speak on behalf of a god

saint A person through whom God has performed miracles, according to the Christian Church

shrine A small area or structure dedicated to a god or saint

slang An informal type of language that is made up of interesting, colorful words. Slang changes over time.

vineyard An orchard where grapes are grown

 # Index

1 2 3 4 5 6 7 8 9 0 Printed in the USA 5 4 3 2 1 0 9 8 7 6